Fast Start Guide - How to Save Money on Prescription Drugs

Diana Loera

Needless to say, you should always check with your doctor or health professional regarding any medical related questions. This book is not meant to diagnose or advise regarding health or medications.

Other Books by Diana Loera

12 Extra Special Summer Dessert Fondue Recipes http://tinyurl.com/q7gpgw8

14 Extra Special Winter Holidays Fondue Recipes http://tinyurl.com/lkebggx

Awesome Thanksgiving Leftovers Revive Guide http://tinyurl.com/prxjayg

Best 100 Calorie or Less Dessert Recipes http://tinyurl.com/pn5b46c

Best Bacon Infused Dessert Recipes: 20 Mouthwatering Delicious Desserts Infused with Bacon http://tinyurl.com/owxo3pl

Best Copycat Recipes on the Planet http://tinyurl.com/pcuj24q

Coca Cola Ham, Coca Cola Cake and Other Coca Cola Recipes http://tinyurl.com/pp2wvhz

Party Time Chicken Wing Recipes http://tinyurl.com/ohsc9x8

Summertime Sangria http://tinyurl.com/oxnlnhm

Please visit www.LoeraPublishingLLC.com to see our complete selection of books. Topics include cooking, travel, recipes, how to, non- fiction and more.

Table of Contents

Introduction

With the economy being on a wild rollercoaster ride for several years, more and more people are feeling the agony of trying to make ends meet.

Add to this problem, an aging Baby Boomer crowd and a rise in prescription needed illnesses and you have a snapshot of the problem more and more Americans are facing daily.

You may be a senior citizen with a set budget who is seeing your prescription price go up or a caregiver for an older family member who is struggling to fit ever increasing prescription prices into your budget.

You may be a middle aged person with growing health issues or a parent with a child in need of prescriptions.

Regardless of who you are or your situation, if you have opened this book, most likely you are facing the growing problem of skyrocketing pharmaceuticals and trying to find a way to save money on prescriptions.

This book came about as my own mother faced the prescription hike nightmare.

This is actually a two part story but I think well worth briefly telling what led up to this book as you may also be in the same situation or a similar one -

My mother is retired and on a set pension. One month her monthly pension check was not auto deposited into her bank account. After a day or two I called the bank and found out, from an employee that off the record, countless others hadn't received their monthly stipend from the same company. It was a local company here in our community that probably employs the most people in our small city.

Calls to my mother's former employer went to a voicemail. None of those calls were returned.

Almost two weeks later she received a form letter that the pension funds had not panned out as planned and quite basically, she was shafted. They, whoever "they" was, had made some bad investment choices with the money and now, well, sorry but you were out of luck.

She was told, via the form letter, she would receive a settlement that was a portion of the pension she was to receive and she was responsible for finding a place to put this money, or within thirty days, the company would issue a check for the amount, minus taxes.

We went to the bank and the bank manager kindly expedited the matter and helped us with all the paperwork so she could place the money into a fund to shelter it from a one lump sum tax payment. It was a very stressful ordeal for my mother to say the least.

This story doesn't end here though.

Please keep in mind that my mother used a good portion of her pension for her medications. So for several months, my husband and I had to foot the bill for her medicines and her monthly bills.

About two months after the pension debacle, my mother received the pittance of her original pension.

The bank helped her set it up so she would receive monthly payments, as she had with her pension. The only difference being the amount was considerably less, making the monthly amount considerably less and the length of times that she would have the monthly amount even less. As I write this book, she has at best one more year of the highly reduced payment coming in and then will be fully dependent upon social security.

Blow number two came not soon after that ordeal. Upon going to see her doctor, she was informed her one prescription which had been around five dollars a month was now not being manufactured. There was a replacement – with her double insurance it was fifty dollars a month.

A visit to the pharmacy brought the news that we weren't the only ones up in arms over this change.

This is when we decided enough of the madness – we were going to look at the best way to save money on prescriptions and protect ourselves with an arsenal of information.

We found out that there are ways to get prescriptions at lower prices and sometimes even at no cost.

There are ways to pay less in co-pays and ways to get the lowest price on prescriptions and in some case get the needed medicines at no cost.

Some of the ways do take a bit of investigating on your part but when you see that you can save hundreds and maybe thousands a year, a little research is well worth it.

People, just like you, just like me, just like my mom are being put in a bad situation. Did you know that in January 2015, the U.S. Center for Disease Control and Prevention reported that nearly one in ten adults don't take their medications as prescribed because they can't afford them?

This fact is very scary to say the least.

My husband and I now have to help my mom financially and we all know as she ages, her prescriptions will increase.

In this book, I've outlined some options to help you cut your prescription costs.

Everyone's situation is different but I do hope that you find an idea or two to help you control skyrocketing prescription costs.

Some of my tips may not work for you. Some tips may be things you have already thought of.

Some of my tips may require some effort on your part but now you at least have met someone, through this book who has taken the steps and you have an idea what to expect.

Our health care system is in a full blown crisis and I do not see it improving any time soon. I understand the struggle that more and more people face every day when it comes to skyrocketing medication costs and insurance companies seeming less and less willing to cover medications. Please know you are not alone in this matter.

I wish you the very best and hope the information in this book is helpful to you.

Sincerely,

Diana

Price Comparisons

You may be very surprised to find out the difference in the cost of a prescription from one place to another.

While it may be convenient to pick up your prescription at the local pharmacy, you may be surprised at the deeper discount that you may get for the same prescription at a wholesale club such as Sam's Club or Costco.

You do not have to belong to the Costco club to use their pharmacy services.

WalMart and Target pharmacies are two more worth checking out.

This is where it gets interesting though – many stores will match prices. So if the lowest price for your prescription is at a wholesale club on the other side of town, you may not need to drive there.

Find out from your regular pharmacy if they will match or beat the price you have from the other store and what is needed to do so.

By the way – don't take no for an answer. If you are told no they don't match prices, call their corporate office and ask them to verify that they do Not match prices.

With competition at an all -time high for pharmaceutical sales, the odds are good that you'll be successful with price comparing and price matching.

But we aren't going to stop there as the next three tips may be able to be combined with this tip to generate more savings.

Tip 2

Loyalty cards

Many stores now offer a loyalty card. It is sometimes called a rewards card.

It is free. When you have the card and make purchases you will accrue points, get discounts or a combination of both.

Walgreens is our local drugstore. When I buy things – from chips to shampoo and everything in between, I show my loyalty card.

The cashier scans it and I accrue points.

Sometimes they have really good specials such as buy a specific shampoo and get another thousand or so points.

When you have accrued a set amount of points, you receive five dollars off your order.

I carry the loyalty card on my keyring and remember to use it every time I am in Walgreens.

Check with your local sores with pharmacies and see what type of loyalty program that they offer.

Tip 3

Coupons

If a pharmacy is having a grand opening many times they will offer a coupon for $5 or $10 off your new or transferred prescription so that they can get a new customer.

Other times you will see an established pharmacy offer a coupon for similar savings as above.

I have switched pharmacies several times, jockeying between two pharmacies, one in a grocery store that had a drug store attached and one in a stand - alone drugstore. They are located a stone's throw apart from each other.

As is sometimes the case, an employee at one of the stores said to me that I could not keep transferring back and forth. I examined the coupon and it did not state anything about a limit. I pointed this out to the employee.

I will add that a few months later, the coupon did have a new policy regarding transfers.

That was fine with me but the point being made is do not go along with something just because the employee states it is true.

Ask to see where this is written and escalate the matter as needed. I will discuss another example of this occurring later in this book.

Sometimes employees are not schooled on how to do discounts or how a coupon works. I've ran into this situation on an increasing basis the past couple years from using a coupon at a department store to save $10 on an item $10 or more to using an in store coupon at the grocery store to getting a rain check. In those cases the employees were not reading the coupon correctly and tried to deny applying it to my purchase.

I've ran into it at two well- known discount stores this summer –in both cases shoppers wanted to use the store's phone app for a discount that the store was promoting and both times the employee was totally untrained on what to do.

In one of the two stores, the manager was called and she didn't know how to process the discount either.

You can either slink away or you can contact their corporate office and ensure that you receive the savings you're entitled to.

You may need to work your way up the management chain of command but just in these examples, you've seen a considerable amount of savings that would have been lost if the customer hadn't pursued the matter.

It isn't just about getting the best price on your prescription but also about being a savvy shopper regarding all your of your shopping.

Every dollar adds up especially if you're on a fixed income budget.

90 day supply

I found this tip to be a money saver that many people do not use as they aren't aware of it.

If you have a co-pay insurance plan, switching to a 90 day supply versus 30 day supply may eliminate two of the co-pay costs.

For example – if your co-pay is three dollars, if you get a 90 day supply versus a 30 day supply, you may be able to save six dollars. This will depend upon your insurance but is definitely a way to save money if you can utilize it.

If you do not have a co-pay, switching to a 90 day supply still saves you the time and gas to go two more times versus once.

Tip 5

Grants and other ways to receive free or discounted prescription medications

There are now a lot of programs being offered to help reduce or even eliminate the cost of your prescription.

Pharmaceutical companies hand out billions of dollars in medications to people who are in need and who qualify.

Financial help from pharmaceutical companies is generally for brand-name drugs that don't have generic equivalents.

Many have relatively generous thresholds that include middle-class families so please do not think these programs are only for those with very low incomes.

If you have prescription drug coverage but can't afford your co-pay, there are programs that may help with that, too.

A few helpful websites for financial assistance include

Partnership for Prescription Assistance www.pparx.org

Patient Services Inc. www.PatientServicesInc.org

Patient Advocate Foundation's National Financial Resource Directory
www.PatientAdvocate.org

Do not accept a cashier's verbal input on coupons, prescriptions covered etc.

You need to be a savvy shopper. As we discussed earlier, if you use a coupon to transfer a prescription and a cashier states you can't do so a second time, if the coupon doesn't state that you can't do it, then question their assumption.

You can do this in a nice way, and I'm sure you will, but you do have the right to question something that is not backed by a written statement issued by the corporate office.

On a similar note, sometimes you may be told that your medication is not covered by your insurance.

I learned this lesson the hard way several years ago when I refilled a prescription and the pharmacy tech told me it wasn't covered under my insurance. I paid full price versus a co-pay.

I called the insurance company, found out that it was covered. Every time for the next three or four months, I had to argue with the pharmacy technician regarding the prescription being covered. It was embarrassing and I dreaded going in to pick up my prescription.

Finally, one day I had enough. I firmly asked for the manager and explained that every month for several months this incident happened and I would be happy to take my business to the pharmacy down the street.

I received a profuse apology and never had a problem filling that prescription again.

On a similar note, if you are told your insurance will not cover your medication, and you find out the pharmacist or pharmacy technician is correct, ask if the insurance will cover a generic version of it.

Don't ever assume the pharmacist or pharmacy technician will voluntarily tell you this information.

Many pharmacies are understaffed and unless you ask for information, the employee may not even think to look into the matter for you.

Generic versus name brand

You may be surprised to find that in many cases if you do not ask your doctor to prescribe a generic version, he or she will write a prescription for an often much higher priced name brand.

Also, in some cases, if there are two name brands for the doctor to choose from, one of the two may have a generic option that is much lower priced than the other generic option.

I then go one step further – I always ask the pharmacist if there is a similar medicine under a different name, and then if so, what is the pricing for that name brand and that generic version.

Pharmaceutical sales reps visit your doctor's office and they may promote one brand over another.

If your doctor declines to prescribe a generic version, ask why.   Are there proven adverse consequences with the generic version?

It is your right as a patient to know why a doctor prescribes one brand over another.

Do a little research before you fill the prescription.

Check the website of the pharmaceutical company that markets your prescribed medicine. In some cases, they may post a coupon or have an offer of getting the first month free.

You also may want to ask your doctor if he/she is aware of any coupons or cost reducing programs.

This takes us back to the pharmaceutical sales rep again. They may have left coupons or brochures with your doctor for your prescribed medicine so take a moment to ask.

If there is a senior citizen center in the city where you live or a center that treats low income patients, check with one or both to see if they are aware of any coupons or discounts on medications.

This may seem like a bit of work and yes, it is but if you can make two calls and one call results in a way to save even more money on a prescription, the couple minutes that it took you to make the calls could result in saving a substantial amount on your prescription.

Are you using a prescription discount card?

Usually you can acquire one of these cards free. This is because the company often makes a small commission on every prescription you fill.

If a friend or co-worker offers you a discount prescription card, most likely they make a dollar or so for every prescription that you fill. Which personally, that is fine with me as the card saves me money.

The prescription discount card is free and has no activation requirement. All you do is take it in to your local pharmacy, and they will give you the discount.

Once you use it, it is in the system and will be applied toward any prescriptions you get at that pharmacy. You don't have to show it a second time.

If you have pets, there's also companies, often the same one, that offers a free card to get discounts on pet medication.

Again, do your homework. Sometimes the pharmacy may tell you that you will not save money with this card. Instead they will use theirs.

That is the reason you want to do your homework first. This way, you know for sure exactly what you should be saving. Also, in the future, if the price happens to increase, you will not be surprised.

I also suggest asking the pharmacy if they receive compensation every time that you use their card.

The odds are quite high that they do. What it may come down to is if you use their card, they earn a dollar or so for every prescription and if you use your friend's card, your friend earns a dollar or two.

Ask your doctor if he or she has any samples

This tip worked well for my mom until the past year or so. The medical network opened a low income help center and we think that may be where the samples now go as they have been far and few between.

If your doctor doesn't have samples available, and you have an adverse reaction to the medication, there are no refunds on the prescription that you just had filled.

You could ask for a smaller amount of pills but then we go back to the co-pay tip and if you use the one week supply and the medication is fine, you will need to pay your co-pay again for a regular sized refill.

The benefit of getting a sample prior to a prescription is that you'll be able to see how your body is going to tolerate the medication.   State this to your doctor.

'

Tip 11

Stay up to date on what medications that your insurance carrier covers.

This tip comes down to being one step ahead of the game. If your prescription price increases question the increase with the pharmacy. If they say the medication price increased and they are just passing the price along, check elsewhere.

My mother's medication increased three dollars and when I questioned the price, the pharmacy double checked and then lowered it back down.

You may think three dollars so what? Or if you are someone on a fixed budget you may be thinking three dollars a month adds up to almost forty a year and may equal a week's worth of groceries.

If you find your medicine price has increased, mention this to your doctor and ask if there is a lower priced option.

You may recall earlier in this book when I mentioned that the medicine my mother was taking was discontinued and the doctor replaced it with a much higher priced medication. The pharmacy tech told me that we were not the only ones complaining.

Due to my mother standing firm with her doctor that this was just too costly, he found a replacement that was close to the same price as the original.

You need to stay on top of any changes to pricing that your insurance carrier makes. Taking the couple minutes to read any updates that arrive in the mail or in your email may save you from a large, and not good surprise of a price hike.

Tip 12

Over the counter alternatives

This may surprise you but depending upon what your prescription is for, there may be an over the counter option.

My mother went to her doctor when she had toenail fungus. The medication he was going to prescribe was not cheap and her insurance did not cover it. Plus it had some very bad side effects.

She was able to get an over the counter option from a holistic store, recommended by her doctor, for less than twenty dollars. I think it was around twelve dollars.

I have ended up with an over the counter medicine myself but in my case, the medicine was kept behind the pharmacy counter.

The pharmacist told me about it when he saw that my insurance wouldn't cover the cost of what was prescribed. He called my doctor explained the situation and I ended up with the over the counter medication.

You may want to ask your doctor if there is an over the counter alternative. If you have a low co-pay, a prescription may be the better choice. I do suggest asking either way because if your medication is discontinued, you at least know there is another option.

Tip 13

Ordering medications

Did you know that you can have your medication shipped to you?

You know you can save time and money when you buy medicine online or through a mail-order pharmacy, but still you wonder: Is the seller legit and are the drugs safe?

Follow these steps to make sure you're getting a good deal.

1. Be cautious of a super-bargain.

If it's too good to be true, it probably is.

An extremely low price can be a sign that there's something fishy going on. For example, if you normally pay $100 for your medicine and you can get it for $5, be careful. It could mean the drugs are sold outside the U.S. and aren't approved by the FDA.

2. Check for the VIPPS seal.

When you go to a pharmacy's web site, look for a seal that says VIPPS. It stands for "Verified Internet Pharmacy Practice Sites." If it's there, it means the site was screened and approved by the NABP- National Association of Boards of Pharmacy. This is a group that encourages safety standards for pharmacies.

3. Make sure the company is licensed and based in the U.S.

An online or mail-order pharmacy should be located in this country. Check if it's licensed or registered by the state where it's based. To find out, go to the web site of the NABP.

You can also look for licensing information on the online pharmacy's web site. If they don't list it, be wary as that is usually a warning sign that this is not an ideal place to shop.

4. Check that the company has a pharmacist on staff.

You should be able to talk with a pharmacist by phone, by email, or online. There should be a toll free number listed on the site so you can contact a pharmacist if you have a question about your medication just like you would be able to do at your local pharmacy.

If you do start to use a mail order pharmacy, it is best to fill all your prescriptions through the same one so your pharmacist can watch for possible problematic drug combinations or other problems.

5. Only use pharmacies that require a prescription from your doctor or other licensed professional. If the pharmacy doesn't ask for a prescription this is a red flag.

6. Look at privacy policies on the website or in the marketing materials.

The company should not be selling your personal information unless you are notified and agree to allow them to do so.

7. Keep your personal information safe.

Do not give out your social security number, personal medical history, date of birth or personal medical information unless you are certain the company is legit and even then, I would be hesitant regarding sharing information with them except that which is absolutely relevant.

This list isn't meant to scare you away from the idea of mail order. Unfortunately there are some bad apples in the online and mail order world and you need to use caution.

Tip 14

Partnership for Prescription Alliance

This group contains a database of options. You just type in either your zip code or your medications and options pop up.

The site address is www.pparx.org I will say, it is a very user friendly site.

It did not offer much as far as help in my search as even though we are located about 40 miles away from Chicago, when I entered my zip code, I was matched with clinics in a rather bad area in Illinois and none in Indiana where I live.

I did expect to find matches in Indiana and also closer to my home but I wouldn't eliminate this site as one to look at as your results may be much better than mine.

As mentioned, the site is user-friendly and has access to almost 500 public and private programs.

Tip 15
As seen on TV – Buyer beware

I have to add this tip as my background is advertising.

The pharmaceutical companies have really jumped on the advertising bandwagon. They spent millions of dollars on TV and radio advertising, as well as newsprint, Internet, magazine and direct mail ads.

As with any advertiser, their goal is to tempt you to buy or in this case, go to your doctor and ask about this medication.

Many times, the symptoms listed are rather general and could apply to many different situations. The new disorders are also popping up left and right.

If you see an ad on TV for a new drug, don't be swept up in the ad and think this is a medication that you need.

Do your homework and discuss the medication and the side effects of it with your doctor.

Be certain that you really need it versus having an added expense each month.

Tip 16

Have a yearly review of your medications with your doctor.

Medications are changing daily. Once a year, ask your doctor to go over the list of medications that you are taking.

Are there better options?   Perhaps a generic version is now available for one of your medications.

Do you need to be taking all your medications or are there any that can be changed or eliminated?

Medicare Part D coverage gap

If you are on the Medicare Part D program there are coverage gaps that occur when you reach a certain spend on medications.

According to www.Medicare.gov most Medicare Prescription Drug Plans have a coverage gap (also called the "donut hole"). This means there's a temporary limit on what the drug plan will cover for drugs.

Not everyone will enter the coverage gap. The coverage gap begins after you and your drug plan have spent a certain amount for covered drugs. In 2015, once you and your plan have spent $2,960 on covered drugs (the combined amount plus your deductible), you're in the coverage gap. In 2016, once you and your plan have spent $3,310 on covered drugs, you're in the coverage gap. This amount may change each year. Also, people with Medicare who get Extra Help paying Part D costs won't enter the coverage gap.

Once you reach the coverage gap in 2015, you'll pay 45% of the plan's cost for covered brand-name prescription drugs. You get these savings if you buy your prescriptions at a pharmacy or order them through the mail. The discount will come off of the price that your plans has set with the pharmacy for that specific drug.

Although you'll only pay 45% of the price for the brand-name drug in 2015, 95% of the price—what you pay plus the 50% manufacturer discount payment—will count as out-of-pocket costs which will help you get out of the coverage gap. What the drug plan pays toward the drug cost (5% of the price) and what the drug plan pays toward the dispensing fee (55% of the fee) aren't counted toward your out-of-pocket spending.

Medicare site – for more information about the coverage gap

https://www.medicare.gov/part-d/costs/coverage-gap/part-d-coverage-gap.html

The link below is for a Medicare Part D coverage gap calculator

http://www.q1medicare.com/PartD-PartDCoverageGapCalculator15Xphp.php

This is a resource for those states that operate within the Medicare program.
https://www.medicare.gov/pharmaceutical-assistance-program/state-programs.aspx

When I began researching this site, I noticed that not all fifty states are participating.

See if your state is participating and what the requirements are. This is yet another strategy that can help you in paying drug plan premiums.

What to Do if You Have Medical Bills Not Covered by Insurance or if You Don't Have Insurance

While I don't want to get in to a political debate, I have heard countless stories from people who do not qualify for government assisted health insurance and cannot afford health insurance on their own.

The premiums skyrocketed after Obama Care was put into place. I think there needs to be some sort of regulation as many policies now have incredibly high monthly premiums and deductibles – why? Because they know Americans are supposed to have health insurance so they, in my opinion, are taking advantage of people and skyrocketing the rates.

Then, they refuse to pay for simple things such as breathing tubes needed during surgery. The patient is then stuck with the bill.

If you have found yourself facing a gut wrenching stack of medical bills, take a deep breath and let's look at options that may help you reduce all or most of the bills.

To begin – purchase a folder. The cheap ones that kids use for school work is fine. You just need to be very organized during this process as you'll see as we continue.

When one has surgery, bills will start pouring in. Depending upon the hospital, you may have bills from the hospital, the doctor, the x-ray reader, the anesthesiologist and several other people.

Contact social services at the hospital and tell them that you do not have health insurance. Most likely, if you have stated that you do not have health insurance when you are admitted, social services will contact you while you are in the hospital but if they don't, you need to contact them.

You will be asked to apply for Medicaid and even if your income is too high, you do need to at least apply.

As soon as you start receiving the medical bills, call each and every company/doctor that has sent a bill.

On the outside of the bill envelope – write the date, time, name of person that you speak with and rep ID if they have one.

You will be telling that person that you have received the bill and the hospital has helped you apply for Medicaid.

The person on the other end of the phone should then note this on your account. They generally then allow 30-90 days for you to find out of Medicaid will be paying.

Once you are done with your call, add any notes about the call such as the person that you spoke with said she would note it on your account and asked you to update them in 60 days.

Then put bill and envelope with your notes back in your medical bills folder.

If you are approved for Medicaid, the parties will be paid via Medicaid.

If Medicaid denies payment, often hospitals have a charity program that you can apply to receive.

You will usually need tax returns, information on your monthly expenses, monthly income and a letter stating why you are requesting assistance.

Each hospital is different and the charity program may have a set day in which applicants are reviewed. They may have a set budget regarding how many cases they will review and help.

You will again need to contact all the parties who sent a bill and let them know you have applied for the hospital's assistance program.

Some may tell you that they will follow suit – so if the hospital waives 80 percent of your bill, they will do so also.

Others may request tax returns and other documents to determine if they will offer a reduction.

It is fully worth taking an hour or more to compile these documents as you may be looking at over 20,000 in unpaid medical bills if not more.

Handy tip – if you have to make copies of tax returns etc. Make at least 3 or 4 copies of each as the odds are good you may need more copies. Sometimes more pages copied provides a deeper copy savings cost too. You may find that each medical provider needs a copy or it is possible for your submission to get lost along the processing path.

If you set up a payment plan, do not feel forced to pay more than you can comfortably pay. You are better off committing to 25 dollars a month than 100 a month if you know with certainty you can come up with 25 each month. You can always send more money.

Do not feel forced to put the bill on your credit card or to take out a loan.

If you are still making payments almost a year later, ask the billing contact if they would accept a reduced payoff – providing that you can swing it.

For example, with a 2000 dollar open balance, I found out that Medicaid, had the person qualified, would have only paid the bill up to 600.00. Interesting isn't it – Medicaid had you qualified, would have paid the provider 600 dollars and they would have accepted it.

But as the person did not qualify for Medicaid, he then had a 2000 remaining balance and this was after the medical provider had discounted the bill due to not having insurance.

The person then asked the doctor's office if they would accept 600 in full which would be 200 a month over 3 months versus 25 a month to pay on the open balance of 2000. In this case, the medical group accepted the offer.

Also, if you are not covered by Medicaid or insurance, tell each medical provider as often they will reduce the bill or in some cases wipe it out.

Just remember, take notes, include the date, time and name of person that you talked with.

If later, a collection agency starts calling or contact you, tell them you have been in constant communication with the medical provider.

Then call the medical provider and state – On such and such date I spoke with the name of a person. Our agreement was that we would not make any payments until Medicaid decided if they were paying or not – or whatever your agreement was.

If you are to the point of making payments – ask the person if they now want you to pay the collection company or their office. I would also try to get out of something now going through a collection agency as there is n need for that to be done if you have kept your end of the agreement.

I have seen people pay a collection agency and a medical office for the same bill and then later each company deny there was a double payment.

I've also seen supposed collection queries show up on credit reports years after when in fact the bill was dismissed, reduced or paid directly.

It is frustrating to have to micromanage paying off medical bills but unfortunately it is something you need to do.

Don't ever let anyone make you feel like it is your fault for not having insurance. It is a shame that in this country many hard working people make too much money to qualify for Medicaid yet the Obama Care fiasco has caused insurance premiums to skyrocket – yet is not being regulated.

Resources

Following are numerous resources that I have found online or that have been shared with me by others.

Cancer Patients Resources

1. Cancer Financial Assistance Coalition – www.cancerfac.org – This is a group of national organizations that provide financial help.

2. The Healthwell Foundation – http://www.healthwellfoundation.org – This foundation provides financial assistance to cover co-payments, premiums, and deductibles for certain medications and therapies. 800-675-8416.

3. The Patient Access Network Foundation – www.panfoundation.org – This foundation assists patients with out-of-pocket costs associated with their treatment. 866-316-7263.

4. The National Children's Cancer Society – www.thenccs.org – This organization has a transportation fund and an emergency assistance fund, and they have a scholarship titled Beyond the Cure, which is a survivorship program. 314-241-1600.

5. Cancer Care – www.cancercare.org – This organization provides financial assistance designed to help with cancer-related costs and even pain medication.

6. Manage Cancer – www.managecancer.org – This site contains links and resources. Whether it is financial assistance to support, education, and even information for your loved ones, you will find it there.

7. Patient Advocate Foundation – https://www.copays.org/diseases – Find information on co-pay relief for various diseases. Go to the link, choose your particular disease or illness, and determine what is available and how to apply. 1-866-512-3861.

8. Prostate Cancer Foundation – http://www.pcf.org/site/c.leJRIROrEpH/b.5856497/k.F968/Financial_Resources.htm – They have resources available to help patients with screening, cost of treatment, and medical debt.

1. The Assist Fund – www.assistancefund.org – This fund provides financial support to chronically ill patients with high-cost of medications. 855-845-3663.

2. Good Days (formerly Chronic Disease Fund) – www.gooddaysfromcdf.org – They help patients suffering from chronic medical conditions, who have limited finances, get access to the medications they need.

3. Patient Services, Inc. – www.patientservicesinc.org – Offers one year of full or partial financial assistance with health insurance premiums and co-payment costs to qualified, chronically ill patients.

4. For patients with rheumatoid arthritis – http://www.encouragefoundation.com/index.jsp

5. For arthritis – http://www.arthritis.org/living-with-arthritis/health-care/paying-for-care/drug-specific-patient-assistance-programs.php Pharmaceutical companies helping with lowering the cost of specific medications

6. Leukemia and Lymphoma Society – http://www.lls.org/support/financial-support – This society has a co-pay assistance program to help toward the cost of insurance co-payments or insurance premium costs for prescription drugs.

7. American Kidney Fund – http://www.kidneyfund.org/ – This fund helps dialysis patients pay for health insurance premiums and other treatment-related expenses.

3 Little Birds 4 Life
http://3littlebirds4life.org/contact-us/need-a-wish/
Cancer-All
Grants wishes to young adults with cancer.

4 Paws for Ability
http://4pawsforability.org/
Childhood Disability, Amputation, Deafness, Assistance Dog
Provides quality service dogs with children with disabilities and veterans who have

Ability Found
http://www.abilityfound.org/AboutUs/How-We-Work.aspx
Cerebral Palsy, Spina Bifida, Spina Bifida, Multiple Sclerosis, Stroke, Spinal Cord Injuries, Spinal Cord Injuries, Cancer - All, Hydrocephalus, Hydrocephalus, Diabetes, Amputation, Lung Diseases - all, Congenital Heart Disease, Disability Requiring Assistive Technology
Provides medical and rehabilitation equipment to individuals who have a medical condition covered by the program. Please note this program does NOT provide diabetic supplies.

Air Charity Network
http://aircharitynetwork.org/
Care Requiring Air Transportation
Provides access to medical air transport.

Alexander Graham Bell Association for the Deaf - Preschool-Aged Financial Aid Program
http://listeningandspokenlanguage.org/Document.aspx?id=270
Hearing Loss
Provides financial assistance for spoken language education to families of children diagnosed with a moderate to profound hearing loss.

Alexander Graham Bell Association for the Deaf - School-Age Financial Aid Program
http://www.agbell.org/Document.aspx?id=271
Hearing Loss
Provides financial assistance for school-related expenses to families of children age 6-21 diagnosed with a moderate to profound hearing loss.

Alternatives in Motion
http://www.alternativesinmotion.org/about
Disability
Provides wheelchairs to individuals who have a disability.

American Academy of Dermatology - Free skin cancer screenings

http://www.aad.org/spot-skin-cancer/what-we-do/free-skin-cancer-screenings
Skin Cancer, Skin Cancer
Provides skin cancer screenings.

American Academy of Facial Plastic and Reconstructive Surgery -FACES OF HONOR Program
http://www.aafprs.org/face-to-face/faces-of-honor/
Injuries to Face, Neck or Head, Scars on Face, Neck or Head
Provides facial plastic and reconstructive surgery to active duty service members and veterans.

American Breast Cancer Foundation - Breast Cancer Assistance Program
http://www.abcf.org/programs/breast-cancer-assistance-program
Breast Cancer
Provides financial and other types of assistance to uninsured individuals who have breast cancer.

American Cancer Society
http://www.cancer.org/index
Cancer - All
Local ACS offices may offer reimbursement for expenses related to cancer treatment during the cancer experience.

American Cancer Society - Wig Banks Program
http://www.cancer.org/treatment/supportprogramsservices/app/resource-detail.aspx?resourceId=54014
Cancer - All
Provides free wigs, accessories, or styling services to individuals diagnosed with cancer through participating salons of the American Cancer Society.

American Sleep Apnea Association - CPAP Assistance Program
http://www.sleepapnea.org/resources/cpap-assistance-program.html
Sleep Apnea, Ventilator or CPAP Dependence
Program provides CPAP therapy equipment for individuals affected by Sleep Apnea.

American Society of Journalists and Authors (ASJA) - Writers Emergency Assistance Fund (WEAF)
http://www.asja.org/for-writers/weaf/
All Diseases, Disability
Provides financial assistance to non-fiction writers who are unable to work because of advanced age, illness, disability, natural disaster, or extraordinary professional crisis.

American Syringomyelia & Chiari Alliance Project (ASAP)
http://www.asap.org/index.php/resources/bjo-equipment/
Syringomyelia, Chiari malformation, Disability Requiring Assistive Technology
Provides financial assistance for medical equipment.

American Transplant Foundation
http://www.americantransplantfoundation.org/programs/pap/
Transplant - All, Organ Donors
Provides financial assistance to transplant patients and living organ donors.

Andre Sobel River of Life Foundation - Everyday Needs Assistance Fund
http://andreriveroflife.org/
Childhood Cancer
Provides financial assistance to single parents of children who have a life threatening illness.

Andrew and Abby Szott Foundation - Gift of Time
http://www.szottfoundation.org/
Childhood Cancer, Childhood Cancer
Provides financial assistance so that one parent, previously working full-time, can stay home with a child with cancer.

Andrew McDonough B+ Foundation
http://bepositive.org/receive_help.php
Chronic/Serious/Life Threatening Illnesses-Children
Provides financial assistance to families with a child who has a critical illness.

Angel Airline Samaritans
http://www.angelairlinesamaritans.org/

Care Requiring Air Transportation, Cancer - All
Provides air transport to individuals needing treatment for cancer.

Angel Flight Veteran - Corporate Headquaters
http://www.angelflightveterans.org/
Care Requiring Air Transportation
Provides air transport to veterans and active-duty military personnel and their families who need treatment

Angel Wheels To Healing
http://www.angel-bus.org/
All Diseases
Provides non-emergency long-distance ground transportation to patients in need.

Arizona Burn Foundation, Inc. - Forever Courage House
http://azburn.org/forever-courage-house/
Burn Injury
A shelter for family members of critically burned patients who are receiving treatment at the Arizona Burn Center and for families of severe trauma patients.

Arms Within Reach Foundation
http://www.armswithinreach.org/application/
Amputation
Provides financial assistance to obtain prosthetic limbs for amputees.

Army Community Service - Exceptional Family Member Program (EFMP)
http://hoodmwr.com/acs/efmp.html#Respite
Behavioral Disorders, Allergies, Autism, Asthma, Developmental Delay, Cancer - All, Diabetes, Limb Prosthesis, Amputation, Schizophrenia, Obsessive Compulsive Disorders, Anxiety Disorders

Provides financial assistance for respite services to military families where an individual has a disability covered by the program.

Assistance Fund, Inc. - Clostridium Difficile Associated Diarrhea (CDAD) Copay Assistance Program
http://theassistancefund.org/patient-services/
Clostridium Difficile, Clostridium Difficile
Provides financial assistance for co-payments for patients who have been diagnosed with Clostridium Difficile Associated Diarrhea (CDAD).

Assistance Fund, Inc. - Cystic Fibrosis Co-pay Assistance Program
http://theassistancefund.org/patient-services/
Cystic Fibrosis
Provides financial assistance for co-payments for patients who have cystic fibrosis.

Assistance Fund, Inc. - Hereditary Angioedema (HAE) Financial Assistance Program
http://theassistancefund.org/patient-services/
Hereditary Angioedema
Provides financial assistance for co-payments for patients who have hereditary angioedema.

Assistance Fund, Inc. - Multiple Sclerosis Premium Assistance Program
http://theassistancefund.org/patient-services/
Multiple Sclerosis
Provides financial assistance for insurance premiums for patients who have multiple sclerosis.

Assistance Fund, Inc. - Parkinson's Co-pay Assistance Program
http://theassistancefund.org/patient-services/
Parkinson's Disease
Provides financial assistance for co-payments for patients who have Idiopathic Parkinson's Disease.

Attain - IVF Refund Program
http://attainivf.attainfertility.com/attain-ivf-flex-plan-overview
Infertility
Program provides individuals facing infertility problems with multiple IVF cycles for a single, discounted fee of up to 40% less than normal price.

Attain - RX Discount Card Program
http://attainivf.attainfertility.com/rx
Infertility
Program provides a discount of up to 75% on fertility medications to individuals facing infertility problems.

Autism Escapes
http://www.autismescapes.org/for-families.php
Autism
Provides financial assistance for travel expenses for children with autism.

Avery's Angels Gastroschisis Foundation - Carepackages
http://averysangels.org/programs/carepackages/

Gastrochisis

Provides care packages to families who have babies born with gastroschisis.

Awake in America - Sleep Study Relief Program

http://awakeinamerica.info/donaterelief/

Sleep Apnea

Helps qualified applicants get a sleep study to diagnose a sleeping disorder.

Baby Quest

http://www.babyquestfoundation.org/index.php?option=com_content&view=article&id=11&Itemid=11

Infertility

Provides financial assistance for treatments that can help preserve future fertility.

Bausch + Lomb - SilSoft Pediatric Patient Assistance Program

http://www.bausch.com/our-products/contact-lenses/lenses-for-cataract-patients/silsoft-and-silsoft-super-contact-lenses

Cataracts

Provides free contact lenses for children who have had cataract surgery where an intraocular lens has not been implanted

Bent But Not Broken

http://bentbutnotbroken.org/resources/financial-assistance-application/

Chronic Fatigue Syndrome

Provides financial assistance to CFS/CFIDS patients and their caregivers.

Blessings Unleashed

http://blessingsunleashed.org/our-dogs/

Autism, Assistance Dog

Provides specially trained assistance dogs to children with autism.

Blooming With Autism

http://www.bloomingwithautism.org/grant-application/

Autism

Provides financial assistance to families with a child who has autism.

Blues Foundation - HART Fund (Handy Artists Relief Trust)

http://www.blues.org/hart/

Dental - All, Chronic, Serious or Life Threatening Illnesses

Provides financial assistance for acute, chronic and preventive medical and dental care as well as funeral and burial expenses for Blues musicians and their families.

Bonei Olam

http://www.boneiolam.org/services.php

Infertility

Provides financial assistance for treatment for individuals who have infertility.

Boston University School of Medicine Scleroderma Program

http://www.bumc.bu.edu/rheumatology/scleroderma/

Scleroderma

Provides patient care to individuals diagnosed with Scleroderma.

Bowman Limb Bank Foundation

http://www.danabowman.com/bank_foundation.php

Amputation

Provides financial assistance to obtain prosthetic limbs for amputees.

Breast Cancer Charities of America - Help Now Fund

http://www.thebreastcancercharities.org/help-now-fund/

Breast Cancer

Provides financial assistance for non-medical expenses to patients with breast cancer.

Breathe 4 Tomorrow

http://breathe4tomorrow.org/application-for-assistance/

Cystic Fibrosis, Cystic Fibrosis

Provides financial assistance to families with a member having cystic fibrosis.

Breathe Believe

http://www.breathebelieve.org/index.php

Cystic Fibrosis, Cystic Fibrosis

Provides financial assistance to individuals who have, or to families where an individual has cystic fibrosis.

Brendan Borek High Tides Memorial Fund (Brendan's Fund)

http://brendansfund.org/family_services/

Childhood Cancer, Childhood Cancer

Provides financial assistance to families with a child who has cancer.

Bright Steps Forward

http://www.brightstepsforward.org/?option=com_content&view=article&id=2&Itemid=2

Cerebral Palsy, Autism, Neurologic/Brain, Nerves, and Seizures - All

Provides financial assistance for medical expenses for children who have a neurological disorders.

Bryon Riesch Paralysis Foundation - Charitable Grants

http://www.brpf.org/Grants/Grants.html

Spinal Cord Injuries, Spinal Cord Injuries, Parkinson's Disease, Amyotrophic Lateral Sclerosis, Stroke, Alzheimer's Disease

Provides financial assistance to purchase equipment and for modifications to individuals who have a spinal cord injury.

Byron Riesch Paralysis Foundation

http://www.brpf.org/Grants/ApplicationCharitableGrants.html

Spinal Cord Injuries, Spinal Cord Injuries, Disability Requiring Assistive Technology

Provides financial assistance to individuals who have, or to families where an individual has a spinal cord injury.

Cameron Siemers Foundation for Hope
http://www.cameronsiemers.org/life-grants/
Chronic, Serious or Life Threatening Illnesses
Provides financial assistance to individuals who have a life-threatening illness.

Cancer Resource Foundation - All4One Breast Form Fund
http://www.cancer1source.org/all4one%E2%84%A2-breast-form-fund
Breast Cancer
Provides financial assistance for breast prosthesis for residents with breast cancer.

Cancer Resource Foundation - All4One Garment Fund
http://www.cancer1source.org/all4one%E2%84%A2-garment-fund
Breast Cancer
Provides financial assistance towards mastectomy bras and other garments for women with breast cancer.

Cancer Resource Foundation - All4One LympheDIVAs Program
http://www.cancer1source.org/all4one%E2%84%A2-lymphedivas%E2%84%A2-program
Breast Cancer, Lymphedema
Provides a LympheDIVA compression sleeve and gauntlet for women with breast cancer.

Cancer Survivors' Fund - Prosthetic Limb Assistance Program
http://www.cancersurvivorsfund.org/Applications/MedicalAssistanceEligibility.htm
Childhood Cancer, Amputation, Limb prosthesis, Childhood Cancer
Provides financial assistance to obtain prosthetic limbs for young adults and children with cancer.

Cancercare - AVONCares
http://www.cancercare.org/financial/information
Breast Cancer
Provides limited financial assistance to individuals with breast cancer.

CancerCare - Get You There
http://www.cancercare.org/financial/information
Breast Cancer
Provides financial assistance for transportation to women with metastatic (stage 4) breast cancer.

CancerCare - Linking A.R.M.S. Program
http://www.cancercare.org/financial/information
Breast Cancer
Provides financial assistance to women with breast cancer.

Canine Assistants
http://www.canineassistants.org/about/our-dogs.html
Disability, Epilepsy, Seizure Disorders, Assistance Dog
Provides services dogs for individuals with a disability or seizure disorder.

Canine Companions for Independence

http://www.cci.org/site/c.cdKGIRNqEmG/b.4010979/k.E0C5/Programs.htm

Disability, Hearing Loss, Assistance Dog

Provides service animals to residents with a disability or hearing impairment.

Canine Partners for Life - Service Dog Program

http://k94life.org/programs/servicedog/

Spina Bifida, Amyotrophic Lateral Sclerosis, Arthritis, Cardiac/Heart/Circulatory - All, Spinal Cord Disorders, Spinal Cord Injuries, Spina Bifida, Stroke, Parkinson's Disease, Muscular Dystrophy, Seizure Disorders, Epilepsy, Spinal Cord Injuries, Muscular Dystrophy, Multiple Sclerosis, Diabetes, Cerebral Palsy, Myasthenia Gravis, Fibromyalgia, Paralysis, Chronic Fatigue Syndrome, Disability, Assistance Dog

Provides service dogs to people with a disability or medical condition covered by the program.

Chai Lifeline - The Joseph & Elsie Listhaus ChaiLink Program

http://www.chailifeline.org/programdetail.php?program=10

Genetic Diseases - All, Childhood Diseases - Chronic, Chronic/Serious/Life Threatening Illnesses-Children

Provides webcam connection and laptop loans to recuperating children with life-threatening disease.

Chelsea Hutchison Foundation

http://www.chelseahutchisonfoundation.org/?q=goals

Seizure Disorders, Epilepsy

Provides seizure-prediction devices and financial assistance for seizure-response dogs for individuals who have epilepsy.

Childhood Leukemia Foundation - Hugs-U-Wear

http://www.clf4kids.org/what-we-do/hugs-u-wear

Leukemia, Leukemia

Provides wigs to children diagnosed with leukemia.

Children with Diabetes Foundation - Supplies for CWDF

http://www.cwdfoundation.org/Supplies.htm

Diabetes

Provides medical supplies for emergency situations to children who have diabetes.

Children's Cancer Recovery Foundation - Helping Hands Fund

http://childrenscancerrecovery.org/programs/helping-hands-fund/

Childhood Cancer, Childhood Cancer

Provides financial assistance to families of children who have cancer.

Children's Liver Association for Support Services (C.L.A.S.S.) Direct Family Support Program
http://www.classkids.org/
Liver Disease - Childhood, Childhood Diseases - Liver
Provides financial assistance for non-medical expenses to families with children who have liver disease.

Christina S. Walsh Breast Cancer Foundation
http://www.christinaswalshbcf.org/about.html
Breast Cancer
Provides financial assistance to individuals who have breast cancer.

Christopher's Haven
http://christophershaven.org/
Childhood Cancer, Childhood Cancer
Provides a home away from home to families with a child who has cancer receiving treatment at Boston's MassGeneral Hospital for Children.

Chronic Disease Fund - Premium Assistance
http://www.gooddaysfromcdf.org/our-mission/programs/
Chronic, Serious or Life Threatening Illnesses
Provides financial assistance for co-payments for medical conditions covered by the program.

Chronic Disease Fund - Travel Assistance
http://www.gooddaysfromcdf.org/our-mission/programs/
Chronic, Serious or Life Threatening Illnesses
Provides financial assistance for travel expenses to residents with chronic, serious or life threatening illnesses.

Cindy Donald Dreams of Recovery Foundation, Inc.
http://www.dreamsofrecovery.org/who-we-are
Paralysis due to Spinal Injury, Traumatic Brain Injury, Spinal Cord Injuries, Spinal Cord Injuries, Traumatic Brain Injury
Provides financial assistance for approved therapy programs and equipment to improve daily life of individuals with paralysis due to spinal cord and brain injury.

Clearity Foundation
http://www.clearityfoundation.org/financialform/financialform.aspx
Ovarian Cancer, Ovarian Cancer
Provides financial assistance for diagnostic tests to women with ovarian cancer.

Cleft Lip & Palate Foundation of Smiles - Weimer Bottle Fund
http://www.cleftsmile.org/programs/weimer-bottle-fund/
Cleft Lip/Palate
Provides baby bottles to families with a child with a cleft lip or palate.

CMMS Deshae Lott Ministries, Inc. - Quality of Life Grants
http://www.deshae.org/cmms/outreach.htm
Disability
Provides financial assistance for quality in-home care to individuals who have a disability.

Colon Cancer Alliance - Blue Note Fund
http://www.ccalliance.org/bluenotefund/index.html
Colorectal Cancer, Colorectal Cancer
Provides financial assistance to patients with colorectal cancer undergoing treatment.

Compass to Care
http://compasstocare.org/help-kids-travel-cancer/
Childhood Cancer
Provides financial assistance for travel expenses to families with a child who has cancer.

Cystic Dreams Fund
http://www.cysticdreamsfund.com/
Cystic Fibrosis, Cystic Fibrosis
Provides financial assistance to individuals who have a cystic fibrosis.

Doggie Does Good
http://www.doggiedoesgood.org/applying-service-dog
Disability, Assistance Dog
Provides service animals to individuals with disabilities.

Dravet Syndrome Foundation - Patient Assistance Grant Program (PAG)
http://www.dravetfoundation.org/programs/patient-assistance-grant-program
Epilepsy, Seizure Disorders, Dravet Syndrome, Disability Requiring Assistive Technology
Provides financial assistance for medical expenses for children who have Dravet syndrome or an associated ion channel epilepsy.

Dream2Walk Foundation
http://dream2walk.org/about-us/application/
Spinal Cord Injuries, Spinal Cord Injuries
Provides financial assistance to individuals who have a spinal cord injury.

Edmond J. Safra Family Lodge at NIH
http://clinicalcenter.nih.gov/familylodge/
Care Requiring Lodging Away From Home
Provides a home away from home for families receiving care at the NIH Clinical Center.

Educated Canines Assisting with Disabiliites (ECAD)
http://ecad1.org/
Disability, Assistance Dog
Provides service animals to individuals with disabilities.

Ella Grace Chiari Foundation - Travel Grant Program
http://defeatchiari.com/resources/travel-grant-program/
Chiari malformation
Provides financial assistance for travel expenses to families with a child who has Chiari malformation

Ellen Meadows Prosthetic Hand Foundation
http://www.ln-4.org/
Amputation
Provides free prosthetic hands for amputees.

Eye Dog Foundation
http://www.eyedogfoundation.org/training.php#qualifications
Visual Impairment, Blindness, Assistance Dog
Provides trained German Shepherd guide dogs to the blind and visually impaired for the enhancement of their safety and independence.

Ferring Fertility - Heart Beat Fertility Preservation Program
https://www.ferringfertility.com/savings/heartbeat/
Cancer - All
Provides financial assistance for fertility preservation necessitated by a recent cancer diagnosis or treatment.

Fertile Action
http://www.fertileaction.org/learning-center/resources/financial-aid/
Cancer - All, Infertility
Provides financial assistance for fertility preservation necessitated by a recent cancer diagnosis or treatment.

Fiat Chrysler - Automobility Program
http://www.fcanorthamerica.com/community/automobility/Pages/Automobility.aspx
Disability
Provides cash reimbursement for vehicle modifications for individuals with a disability.

Fighting Back Scholarship Program
http://www.fightingbacksp.org/index.html
Chronic, Serious or Life Threatening Illnesses
Provides financial assistance for rehabilitation to individuals who have a life changing illness or injury.

FOOTPRINTS in the Sky
http://www.footprintsflights.org/
All Diseases
Provides air transport to individuals needing treatment.

Ford Mobility Program
http://www.fordmobilitymotoring.com/HowToGetStarted/ProgramDetails#.U4Yt6Nwlm60
Disability
Provides cash reimbursement for vehicle modifications for individuals with a disability.

Freedom Eye Dogs
http://freedomguidedogs.org/about-us/
Blindness, Visual Impairment, Assistance Dog
Provides trained guide dogs to the blind and visually impaired for the enhancement of their safety and independence.

Freedom Service Dogs of America
http://www.freedomservicedogs.org/programs/client-dog-teams/
Autism, Traumatic Brain Injury, Spinal Cord Injuries, Cerebral Palsy, Spinal Cord Injuries, Muscular Dystrophy, Multiple Sclerosis, Traumatic Brain Injury, Disability, Assistance Dog
Provides service animals to individuals with disabilities.

Friends of Man
http://www.friendsofman.org/
Disability, Hearing Loss, Visual Impairment
Provides several types of assistance to individuals who have a disabilty, hearing loss,or visual impairment

General Motors Mobility Reimbursement Program
http://www.gmmobility.com/mobility-reimbursements/
Disability
Provides cash reimbursement for vehicle modifications for individuals with a disability.

Generation Rescue - Rescue Family Grant
http://www.generationrescue.org/member-log-in/join-grant/
Autism
Provides financial assistance to families with a child who has autism.

Gia Nicole Angel Foundation
http://www.giafoundation.com/extensions
Childhood Disability, Physical Disability, Chronic/Serious/Life Threatening Illnesses-Children, Cerebral Palsy, Paralysis, Paralysis, Multiple Sclerosis, Spina Bifida, Spina Bifida, Childhood Cancer, Childhood Cancer
Provides financial assistance for children who have a physically disabling condition or a chronic medical condition.

Gift of Hearing Foundation
http://www.giftofhearingfoundation.org/what_we_do/financial_assistance.htm
Hearing Loss, Deafness, Cochlear Implant
Provides financial assistance in obtaining a cochlear implant.

Gilenya Go Program

http://www.gilenya.com/c/ms-pill/go-program

Multiple Sclerosis

Provides free and comprehensive support to people who have multiple sclerosis and have been prescribed GILENYA.

Give an Hour

http://www.giveanhour.org/Home.aspx

Post-traumatic Stress Disorder, Addiction, Alcohol dependence, Children with a parent wounded, disabled or killed in military service, Depression, Sexual Violence, Anxiety Disorders, Aggression, Bereavement

Provides free mental health counseling to U.S. military personnel and their families affected by the conflicts in Iraq and Afghanistan.

Global Medical Relief Fund (GMRF)

http://www.gmrfchildren.org/

Burn Injury, Injury, Blindness, Amputation

Provides assistance to children who are missing or have lost the use of limbs or eyes, or have been severely burned, or have been injured due to war, natural disaster or illness.

Good Charity, Inc. - Autistic Society Fund

http://www.goodcharityfund.org/the-autistic-society-fund-page/

Autism

Provides financial assistance to families with a child who has autism.

Good Charity, Inc. - Children's Leukemia of America Fund

http://www.goodcharityfund.org/childrens-leukemia-of-america-fund-page/

Childhood Cancer, Leukemia, Leukemia, Childhood Cancer

Provides financial assistance to families with a child who has cancer or leukemia.

Gridiron Heroes SCI Organization

http://www.gridironheroes.org/about.asp

Spinal Cord Injuries, Spinal Cord Injuries

Provides assistance to those with spinal cord injury sustained during high school football games.

Grifols PatientCare Program - Grifols Assurance for Patients (GAP) Program

http://www.grifolspatientcare.com/pcProgram.html

Primary Immune Deficiency

Provides eligible patients with access to Grifols' coagulation products.

Grifols PatientCare Program - Grifols Patient Assistance (GPA) Program

http://www.grifolspatientcare.com/pcProgram.html

Primary Immune Deficiency

Provides eligible patients with access to Grifols' coagulation products.

Guide Dog Foundation for the Blind, Inc.

http://www.guidedog.org/content.aspx?id=288

Blindness, Assistance Dog

Provides trained guide dogs to the blind and visually impaired for the enhancement of their safety and independence.

Guide Dogs for the Blind

http://www.guidedogs.com/site/PageServer?pagename=about_overview_faq

Blindness, Visual Impairment, Assistance Dog

Provides trained guide dogs to the blind and visually impaired for the enhancement of their safety and independence.

Guiding Eyes for the Blind

http://www.guidingeyes.org/prospective-students/guide-dog-services/how-to-apply/

Blindness, Visual Impairment, Assistance Dog

Provides trained guide dogs to the blind and visually impaired for the enhancement of their safety and independence.

HAE Hope/Dyax Corp.- Dyax HAE Diagnostic Testing Refund Program

https://www.haehope.com/diagnose/get-tested-for-hae

Hereditary Angioedema

Program offers diagnostic testing refunds for out-of-pocket costs related with Hereditary Angioedema (HAE).

Harboring Hearts Housing

http://www.harboringhearts.org/how-we-help/housing-facilities/

Heart Condition, Cardiac/Heart/Circulatory - All

Provides a home away from home to caregivers and cardiac patients receiving treatment in New York City.

HearUSA

http://hearusa.com/

Hearing Loss

Provides FREE hearing checkups and free 60-day hearing aid trail for individuals with hearing problems.

Heavenly Hats

http://www.heavenlyhats.com/

Hair Loss, Hair Loss - Chemotherapy Induced

Provides hats for patients who lose their hair due to cancer treatment or other medical condition which may cause hair loss.

Helping Hands: Monkey Helpers for the Disabled

http://www.monkeyhelpers.org/our-programs/placement

Disability - Mobility, Paralysis, Mobility Disability

Provides placement of specially trained capuchin monkeys with people who are paralyzed, or who suffer other severe mobility impairments.

Hemophilia Federation of America - Helping Hands Program
http://www.hemophiliafed.org/programs/helping-hands/helping-hands-program/
Hemophilia, Von Willebrand Disease, Hemophilia
Provides financial assistance for emergency situations for individuals with hemophilia or von Willebrands.

Hendrick Marrow Program of the Be The Match Foundation - Charlotte
http://bethematch.org/About-Us/Our-partners/Hendrick-Marrow-Program/
Bone Marrow Transplant, Bone Marrow Transplant
Provides financial assistance to marrow transplant patients.

Hope for the Warriors - Critical Care Coordination
http://www.hopeforthewarriors.org/story/18721712/critical-care-coordination
Injury
Provides financial assistance for post-9/11 veterans and their families.

Hope for Young Adults With Cancer (Hope4YAWC) Giving Hope Fund
http://www.hope4yawc.org/giving-hope-fund/
Cancer - All
Provides financial assistance for residents with cancer.

Hope Scarves
http://hopescarves.org/about-us/
Breast Cancer
Provides scarves to individuals with breast cancer.

Hope-Promise-Support Foundation for Scleroderma
http://www.sclerodermasupport.org/
Scleroderma
Provides grants to individuals diagnosed with Scleroderma and their families.

Hospital for Special Surgery - Clinical Trials
https://www.hss.edu/clinical-trials-by-condition.asp#Scleroderma
Provides various clinical trials for individuals diagnosed with Scleroderma.

Hungtington's Disease Assistance Fund (HDAF)
http://hdaf.org/about/
Huntington's Disease, Huntington's Disease
Provides financial assistance to patients who have Huntington's Disease.

Hydro Angels Over America - Hydro Health Program
http://www.hydroangelsoveramerica.org/hydro-health.html
Hydrocephalus, Hydrocephalus
Provides financial assistance to individuals and families with hydrocephalus.

Hydro Angels Over America - Project Daisy

http://www.hydroangelsoveramerica.org/project-daisy-video-tribute.html

Hydrocephalus, Hydrocephalus

Provides financial assistance to cover funeral expenses for families with a loss from hydrocephalus.

International Council on Infertility Information Dissemination (INCIID) IVF Scholarship

http://www.inciid.org/scholarship-faq

Infertility

Provides financial assistance for treatments that can help preserve future fertility.

International Hearing Dog, Inc.

http://www.pawsforsilence.org/hearing_dog_faq.aspx

Hearing Loss, Assistance Dog

Provides vouchers to individuals who have the need for an assistance dog.

J. Kiffin Penry Patient Travel Assistance Fund

http://www.epilepsy.com/get-help/services-and-support/patient-assistance/j-kiffin-penry-patient-travel-assistance-fund

Epilepsy, Seizure Disorders

Provides travel expenses assistance for medical care and/or treatment to individuals with or affected by epilepsy/seizure disorder.

Jacob Michael Davis Foundation

http://www.jacobmichaeldavis.org/help.htm

Provides financial assistance to families of children who have cancer.

Jeanne A. Carpenter Epilepsy Legal Defense Fund

http://www.epilepsy.com/get-help/legal-issues

Epilepsy, Seizure Disorders

Provides financial assistance for legal services to individuals who have epilepsy.

Jeffrey Dendy Memorial Camp Fund

http://jordanthomasfoundation.org/who-were-helping/jeffrey-dendy-memorial-camp-fund

Limb Prosthesis

Provides financial assistance to send children with prostheses to camp.

John Hopkins Scleroderma Center - Clinical Trials

http://www.hopkinsscleroderma.org/research/clinical-trials/

Scleroderma

Provides various clinical trials for individuals diagnosed with Scleroderma.

Jordan Thomas Foundation

http://jordanthomasfoundation.org/our-mission

Trauma

Provides financial assistance for recovery and rehabilitation to children that have suffered a traumatic injury.

Joseph Groh Foundation

http://josephgrohfoundation.org/assistance.html

Spinal Cord Injuries, Spinal Cord Injuries, Disability

Provides financial assistance to members and their families who have spinal cord injuries or permanent disabilities in the HVAC/construction industries.

KALBITOR Access - Financial Assistance

http://www.kalbitor.com/patient/patient-support/financial-assistance.html

Hereditary Angioedema

Provides financial assistance to individuals who have hereditary angioedema.

Kalbitor Expanded Copayment Assistance Program

http://www.kalbitor.com/patient/patient-support/financial-assistance.html

Hereditary Angioedema

Provides financial assistance for individuals with hereditary angioedema.

Kelly Brush Foundation - Individual Grant Program

http://www.kellybrushfoundation.org/grants-programs/individual-grant-program/

Spinal Cord Injuries, Spinal Cord Injuries, Paralysis due to Spinal Cord and/or Brain Injury, Disability Requiring Assistive Technology

Provides financial assistance for adaptive sport, recreation and exercise equipment to individuals who have spinal cord injuries.

Kidney & Urology Foundation of America - Patient Emergency Grants

http://www.kidneyurology.org/Patient_Resources/patient_emergency_grants.php

End Stage Renal Disease

Provides financial assistance for emergency situations for residents with End Stage Renal Disease.

Kidney TRUST

https://davitavillagetrust.org/us/

Chronic Renal Insufficiency, End Stage Renal Disease, Dialysis, Kidney Disease

Provides free screenings for individuals who are at risk for kidney disease.

Knitted Knockers

http://www.knittedknockers.info/free_knockers.htm

Breast Cancer

Provides breast prostheses women with breast cancer.

Lambda Legal

http://www.lambdalegal.org/issues/hiv

HIV/AIDS, AIDS

Provides access to legal assistance for individuals with HIV/AIDS.

Laura Hart Burdick Foundation
http://www.laurahartburdickfoundation.com/the-foundation.html
Lung Transplant, Lung Transplant
Provides financial assistance to lung transplant patients.

Lazarex Cancer Foundation
http://www.lazarex.org/helping-you/looking-for-help
Cancer - All
Provides financial assistance to residents with cancer willing to enroll in clinical trials.

Lexiebean Foundation
http://www.lexiebeanfoundation.org/our-service.php
Childhood Cancer, Childhood Cancer
Provides financial and other types of assistance to families with a child who has cancer.

Lindsay Foundation
http://www.lindsayfoundation.org/Guidelines.html
Chronic/Serious/Life Threatening Illnesses-Children
Provides financial and other types of assistance to families with a child who has catastrophic illness.

Live2Thrive
http://www.live2thrive.org/en/program_overview
Cystic Fibrosis, Cystic Fibrosis
Provides free shipments of vitamins and supplements to individuals with cystic fibrosis

Living with Lupus & Fighting Together
http://www.fightinglupus.org/Our-Mission.html
Lupus
Provides financial assistance to individuals who have, or to families where an individual has lupus.

Lois Merrill Foundation for Carcinoid and other Rare Cancers - Medical Assistance Grant
http://www.thelmf.com/#!help/c21kz
Cancers - Rare, Carcinoid Tumors, Carcinoid Tumors
Provides financial assistance for medical expenses and living expenses to individuals with carcinoid cancer or other rare cancers.

Look Good Feel Better
http://lookgoodfeelbetter.org/
Cancer - All
Holds free workshops that teach beauty techniques to patients with cancer.

Lower Extremity Amputation Prevention Program (LEAP)
http://www.hrsa.gov/hansensdisease/leap/
Diabetes, Amputation, Hansen's Disease (Leprosy)
Provides free monofilament for testing neuropathy to individuals who have diabetes mellitus, Hansen's disease, or any condition that results in loss of protective sensation in the feet.

Lucy's Love Bus - Integrative Therapies Program
http://lucyslovebus.org/lucys-children
Childhood Cancer, Childhood Cancer
Provides financial assistance for alternative therapies to families with a child who has cancer.

Lyme Test Access Program (Lyme-TAP)
http://www.lymetap.com/lyme-disease-financial-assitance
Lyme Disease
Provides financial assistance for Lyme-related lab tests.

Lymphoma Research Foundation - T-Cell Lymphoma Transportation Assistance Fund Grant
http://www.lymphoma.org/site/pp.asp?c=bkLTKaOQLmK8E&b=7987191
Lymphoma - Various Types
Provides financial assistance for travel expenses to transplant patients

Mama Mare Breast Cancer Foundation - Survivors Thrive Grant Program
http://www.mamamare.org/survivorsthrive.html
Breast Cancer
Provides financial assistance for breast cancer survivors.

Melonhead Foundation, Inc.
http://www.melonhead.org/
Childhood Cancer, Childhood Cancer
Provides financial assistance to families with a child who has cancer.

Mending Limbs Organization
http://www.mendinglimbs.org/funding-application/
Amputation
Provides financial assistance to obtain prosthetic limbs for amputees.

Mercy Medical Angels
http://mercymedical.org/
Care Requiring Air Transportation
Provides air transport to individuals needing treatment.

Meredith's Miracles Colon Cancer Foundation
http://www.meredithsmiraclesfoundation.org/index.php?option=com_content&view=article&id=12&Itemid=8
Colorectal Cancer, Colorectal Cancer
Provides financial assistance to individuals who have colon cancer.

MIRA Foundation USA
http://www.mirausa.org/get-involved/apply-for-a-dog/
Blindness, Assistance Dog
Provides guide dogs for legally blind children.

Moonlight Fund
http://moonlightfund.org/programs
Burn Injury
Provides financial assistance to individuals who have burn injuries.

Musella Foundation - Brain Tumor Drug Copayment Assistance Program
http://braintumorcopays.org/index.cfm
Glioblastoma Multiforme, Glioblastoma Multiforme
Program provides financial assistance to families who need help covering the cost of certain drugs used to treat brain tumors.

Myriad Pro - Financial Assistance Program
http://www.myriadpro.com/for-your-patients/financial-assistance-programs/
Cancer - hereditary, Hereditary Cancer
Provides financial assistance to uninsured or underinsured individuals who are at risk for cancer.

National Amputation Foundation - Medical Equipment Give-A-Way Program
http://home.comcast.net/~n2fc/natamp/Program_Service.html
Amputation
Provides medical equipment to residents with a amputation.

National Association of Injured & Disabled Workers (NAIDW) - Grants Program
http://www.naidw.org/resources/grant-information/available-grants
Disability, All Diseases, Injury
Provides short-term financial assistance to injured and disabled workers and their families as a result of injury, disability or illness

National Breast and Cervical Cancer Early Detection Program (NBCCEDP)
http://www.cdc.gov/cancer/nbccedp/screenings.htm
Breast Cancer, Cervical Cancer, Cervical Cancer
Provides breast and cervical cancer screenings and follow-up treatment for women.

National Children's Cancer Society - Emergency Assistance Fund
http://www.thenccs.org/financial-assistance
Provides financial assistance to families who have a child with cancer.

National Eye Foundation, Inc. - Eyes On Children
http://www.nationaleyefoundation.org/index.php?option=com_content&view=category&layout=blog&id=37&Itemid=74
Eye - All
Provides eye exams and glasses to children.

National Federation for Ectodermal Dysplasias Treatment Assistance Program
http://nfed.org/index.php/treatment/treatment_assistance_program
Ectodermal Dysplasia, Ectodermal Dysplasia, Ectodermal Dysplasia, Ectodermal Dysplasia
Provides financial assistance for medical care and dental procedures to patients with ectodermal dysplasia syndrome.

National Foundation for Cancer Research - Cancer Patient Assistance Fund (CPAF)
http://www.nfcr.org/cancer-patient-assistance-fund
Provides financial assistance for molecular profiling and targeted cancer therapies.

National GRACE Foundation
http://www.graceamerica.org/aboutus.html
Cancer - All
Provides counseling and navigation of college admissions and financial aid for students and families affected by cancer.

National Heart Lung and Blood Institute - Patient Recruitment for Studies conducted by NHLBI, NIH
http://patientrecruitment.nhlbi.nih.gov/
Sarcoidosis, Aplastic Anemia, Myelodysplastic Syndrome, Leukemia, Lymphoma - Various Types, Paroxysmal Nocturnal Hemoglobinuria, Sickle Cell Disease, Sickle Cell Disease, Cystic Fibrosis, Pulmonary Hypertension, Pulmonary Fibrosis, Asthma, Cancer - All, Multiple Myeloma, Multiple Myeloma, Cystic Fibrosis, Coronary Artery Disease, Peripheral Artery Disease
Provides free treatment, evaluation, and transportation to individuals eligible for clinical trials at NIH.

National Kidney Foundation Florida - Kidney Early Evaluation Program (KEEP)
https://www.kidney.org/offices/nkf-florida
Kidney Disease
Provides health screenings for individuals who are at risk for kidney disease.

National Living Donor Assistance Center (NLDAC)
http://www.livingdonorassistance.org/
Transplant - All, Lung Transplant, Liver Transplant, Kidney Transplant, Lung Transplant, Kidney Transplant
Provides financial assistance to those who want to donate an organ.

National Organization for Rare Disorders (NORD) Disease Specific Assistance Programs - Advanced Renal Cell Carcinoma Second Line Treatment
http://rarediseases.org/for-patients-and-families/help-access-medications/patient-assistance-programs/?pap-type=2#program-list
Kidney Cancer, Kidney Cancer
Provides financial assistance to individuals who have Advanced Renal Cell Carcinoma.

National Organization for Rare Disorders (NORD) Disease Specific Assistance Programs - Congenital Sucrase-Isomaltase (CSID) Premium Insurance Patient Assistance Program

http://rarediseases.org/for-patients-and-families/help-access-medications/patient-assistance-programs/?pap-type=2#program-list

Sucrase-Isomaltase Deficiency

Provides assistance with insurance premiums for individuals diagnosed with Sucrase-Isomaltase Deficiency.

National Organization for Rare Disorders (NORD) Disease Specific Assistance Programs - CTX (Cerebrotendinous Xanthomatosus)

http://rarediseases.org/for-patients-and-families/help-access-medications/patient-assistance-programs/?pap-type=2#program-list

Cerebrotendinous Xanthomatosus

Provides financial assistance to individuals who have CTX (Cerebrotendinous Xanthomatosus).

National Organization for Rare Disorders (NORD) Disease Specific Assistance Programs - Cushing's Syndrome

http://rarediseases.org/for-patients-and-families/help-access-medications/patient-assistance-programs/?pap-type=2#program-list

Cushing's Syndrome

Provides financial assistance to individuals who have Cushing's Syndrome.

National Organization for Rare Disorders (NORD) Disease Specific Assistance Programs - Diamond Blackfan Anemia

http://rarediseases.org/for-patients-and-families/help-access-medications/patient-assistance-programs/?pap-type=2#program-list

Diamond-Blackfan Anemia, Diamond-Blackfan Anemia

Provides financial assistance to individuals who have Diamond Blackfan Anemia.

National Organization for Rare Disorders (NORD) Disease Specific Assistance Programs - Gaucher Disease

http://rarediseases.org/for-patients-and-families/help-access-medications/patient-assistance-programs/?pap-type=2#program-list

Gaucher Disease

Provides financial assistance to individuals who have Gaucher Disease.

National Organization for Rare Disorders (NORD) Disease Specific Assistance Programs - Lysosomal Acid Lipase (LAL) Deficiency

http://rarediseases.org/patients-and-families/patient-assistance

Lysosomal Acid Lipase (LAL) Deficiency

Provides financial assistance to individuals who have lysosomal acid lipase (LAL) deficiency.

National Organization for Rare Disorders (NORD) Disease Specific Assistance Programs - Morquio-IV-A Syndrome

http://rarediseases.org/for-patients-and-families/help-access-medications/patient-assistance-programs/?pap-type=2#program-list

Morquio-IV-A Syndrome

Provides financial assistance to individuals who have Morquio-IV-A Syndrome.

National Organization for Rare Disorders (NORD) Disease Specific Assistance Programs - Mucopolysaccharidosis Type VI (Maroteaux-Lamy Syndrome)

http://rarediseases.org/for-patients-and-families/help-access-medications/patient-assistance-programs/?pap-type=2#program-list

Maroteaux-Lamy Syndrome

Provides financial assistance to individuals who have Maroteaux-Lamy Syndrome.

National Organization for Rare Disorders (NORD) Disease Specific Assistance Programs - N-Acetyl Glutamate Synthetase (NAGS) Deficiency

http://rarediseases.org/for-patients-and-families/help-access-medications/patient-assistance-programs/?pap-type=2#program-list

N-Acetyl Glutamate Synthetase (NAGS) Deficiency, N-Acetyl Glutamate Synthetase (NAGS) Deficiency

Provides financial assistance to individuals who have N-Acetyl Glutamate Synthetase (NAGS) Deficiency.

Nature's One - Medical Hardship Program

http://www.naturesone.com/articles/medical-hardship.html

Autism, Celiac Disease, Cancer - All, Cerebral Palsy, Down Syndrome, Down Syndrome, Cystic Fibrosis, Cystic Fibrosis, Metabolic Disorders

Provides discounts for formula to families with children with serious medical conditions.

Novo Nordisk Health Care - NovoSECURE

https://www.mynovosecure.com/

Hemophilia, Hemophilia - Inhibitors, Hemophilia, Disability Requiring Assistive Technology

Provides financial assistance for medical expenses to individuals who have hemophilia with inhibitors, acquired hemophilia, or Factor VII deficiency.

Novo Nordisk Patient Assistance - "Cornerstones4Care" Diabetes Care

https://www.cornerstones4care.com/patient-assistance-program.html

Diabetes

Provides certain diabetes medications for free.

OneSight Global - North America
http://www.onesight.org/na/about_us/2010_clinic_schedule/
Visual Impairment
Provides healthy vision, eye-wear and sun protection to those in need worldwide.

Operation Liftoff
http://www.operationliftoff.com/Services.html
Care Requiring Air Transportation, Chronic/Serious/Life Threatening Illnesses-Children
Provides medical air transport.

Operation Walk Denver
http://www.opwalkdenver.org/
Hip Replacement, Knee Replacement
Provides free surgery for joint replacements.

Oral Cancer Foundation - Bruce Paltrow Fund
http://oralcancerfoundation.org/paltrowfund/
Oral cancer, Oral cancer
Provides oral cancer screenings and treatment.

Osto Group
http://www.ostogroup.org/
Colostomy, Ileostomy, Urostomy
Provides ostomy supplies to residents.

Oticon Pediatrics National Hearing Aid Loaner Bank Program
http://www.pro.oticonusa.com/pediatrics/clinical-support/oticon-resources/loaner-bank.aspx
Hearing Loss
Loans hearing aids to children who are in need of immediate amplification.

PAF/Komen Treatment Assistance Program Financial Aid Fund
http://ww5.komen.org/News/Patient-Advocate-Foundation-and-Susan-G--Komen-Announce-the-Launch-of-a-Financial-Grant-Program-for-Breast-Cancer-Patients.html
Breast Cancer
Provides financial assistance to women who have breast cancer.

Parker's Purpose Foundation
http://parkerspurpose.net/index.php?page=application-for-assistance
Childhood Disability, Chronic/Serious/Life Threatening Illnesses-Children, Disability - Childhood, Disability - Childhood
Provides financial assistance to families with a child who has a life altering illness or disability.

Patient Advocate Foundation (PAF) - Radiation Co-Payment Small Grant Financial Aid Fund
http://www.patientadvocate.org/about.php?p=910
Prostate Cancer
Provides financial assistance for co-payments covering prescribed radiation therapy to individuals who have a prostrate cancer.

Patient Services, Inc. - Breast Cancer Screening Program
http://www.patientservicesinc.org/For-Patients/Supported-Illnesses/Breast-Cancer-Screening-Program
Breast Cancer
Provides financial assistance for screenings for women who are at risk for breast cancer.

Patient Services, Inc. - MRI Financial Assistance Program for Young Women
http://www.patientservicesinc.org/For-Patients/Supported-Illnesses/Breast-Cancer-Screening-Program
Breast Cancer
Provides financial assistance for an MRI to determine a diagnosis of breast cancer.

Patient Services, Inc. - Premium Assistance Programs
http://www.patientservicesinc.org/For-Patients/Apply
Acromegaly, Alpha-1-Antitrypsin Deficiency, Chronic Inflammatory Demyelinating Polyneuropathy, Complement Mediated Diseases, Fabry Disease, Hemophilia, Hemophilia, Hemophilia - Inhibitors, Insulin-like growth factor (IGF-1) Deficiency, Pompe Disease, MPS-1 Hurler/Scheie, Primary Immune Deficiency, HIV/AIDS, AIDS, Hereditary Angioedema
Provides financial assistance for insurance premiums to individuals with chronic medical illnesses.

Paws With A Cause
http://www.pawswithacause.org/what-we-do/assistance-dogs
Hearing Loss, Autism, Epilepsy, Seizure Disorders, Assistance Dog
Provides assistance dogs for people with physical disabilities, hearing impairment, seizure disorders, or for children with autism.

Pearce Q. Foundation, Inc.
http://www.pearceqfoundation.org/MV.asp
Childhood Cancer, Childhood Cancer
Provides financial assistance to families of children who have cancer.

Pennies from Heaven - Caleb's Foundation
http://www.calebspennies.org/
Chronic/Serious/Life Threatening Illnesses-Children
Provides financial assistance for families of a child with a critical illness recently hospitalized or receiving ongoing medical treatment

Pervis Jackson Jr Autism Foundation
http://www.pjjraf.org/mission.htm
Autism, Childhood Disability
Provides financial assistance to families with a child who has autism or disability.

Pink Fund
http://thepinkfund.org/
Breast Cancer
Provides financial assistance to individuals who have breast cancer undergoing treatment or are in early recovery from treatment.

PKU Foundation - Standing In the Gap - Formula Assistance
http://www.pkufoundation.com/programs.html
Phenylketonuria
Provides metabolic formula to individuals born with phenylketonuria (PKU).

Project Sloopy
http://projectsloopy.com/
Children with Special Needs
Provides financial assistance for gently used equipment and medical supplies to familes with a child with special needs.

Relief Foundation
http://www.relief-foundation.org/mission.html

Provides financial assistance to individuals diagnosed with Scleroderma and their families.

Rogers Memorial Hospital Foundation (fka Anxiety Disorders Foundation)
http://www.anxietydisordersfoundation.org/
Obsessive Compulsive Disorders, Anxiety Disorders
Provides financial assistance for treatment to individuals who have anxiety disorders and obsessive compulsive disorders.

Rx Outreach - Diabetes Supplies Program
http://www.rxoutreach.org/diabetic/
Diabetes
Provides diabetes care products to individuals who have diabetes.

Ryan Scott Kappes Foundation
http://www.rskfoundation.org/contact.php
Chronic/Serious/Life Threatening Illnesses-Children
Provides financial assistance to help offset the costs associated with a lengthy hospital stay, to families with a child who has a critical illness.

Second Chance for Life
http://www.secondchanceforlife.org/missionvalues.htm
Transplant - All
Provides emergency housing assistance and transportation for transplant patients.

Second Wind Lung Transplant Association - Financial Assistance Program
http://www.2ndwind.org/financial-assistance/index.html
Lung Transplant, Lung Transplant
Provides financial assistance for emergency situations to lung transplant patients.

Short Bowel Syndrome Foundation - The Hardship Award
http://www.shortbowelfoundation.org/index.php/sbscommunity/hardship-awards
Short Bowel Syndrome
Provides financial assistance to individuals with short bowel syndrome.

Sisters Network, Inc. - Breast Cancer Assistance Program (BCAP)
http://www.sistersnetworkinc.org/programs.html
Breast Cancer
Provides several types of assistance to African-American women with breast cancer.

Skin Cancer Assistance for Reconstructive Surgery (SCARS)
http://www.skincancer-scars.com/our-mission.php
Skin Cancer, Skin Cancer
Provides facial plastic and reconstructive surgery to skin cancer survivors.

Small Steps In Speech
http://www.smallstepsinspeech.org/grant-application/individuals/
Apraxia, Disability Requiring Assistive Technology
Provides financial assistance for language therapy to families with a child who has apraxia of speech.

Smile for a Lifetime Orthodontic Foundation
http://s4l.org/Home/tabid/55/Default.aspx
Dental - Children
Provides financial assistance for dental procedures for children.

Smiles For Sophia Forever
http://smilesforsophieforever.org/WhoWeveHelped/ApplyforaGrant.aspx
Brain Cancer/Tumors, Brain Cancer/Tumors
Provides financial assistance families of children who have a brain tumor.

Special Kids Fund
http://www.specialkidsfund.org/wheelchair/
Disability - Childhood
Provides financial assistance for vehicle modifications to individuals who have a disability.

Spinal Cord Opportunities for Rehabilitation Endowment (SCORE)
http://www.scorefund.org/
Spinal Cord Injuries, Spinal Cord Injuries
Provides financial assistance to individuals who have a spinal cord injury.

St. Christopher Truckers Development & Relief Fund
http://truckersfund.com/
All Diseases, Injury, Chronic, Serious or Life Threatening Illnesses
Provides financial assistance to truck drivers and their families who are experiencing catastrophic illness or injury.

St. Jude Children's Research Hospital
http://www.stjude.org/stjude/v/index.jsp?vgnextoid=f87d4c2a71fca210VgnVCM1000001e0215acR CRD
Childhood Cancer, Childhood Cancer
Provides free treatment, travel and lodging for eligible children diagnosed with cancer.

Summit Assistance Dogs
http://summitdogs.org/application-process/
Hearing Loss, Disability - Physical, Assistance Dog
Provides assistance dogs for people with physical disabilities or hearing loss.

Support Dogs, Inc. - Assistance Dogs
http://www.supportdogs.org/Programs/Assistance-Dogs
Physical Disability, Post-traumatic Stress Disorder, Hearing Loss, Assistance Dog
Provides service dogs for individuals with qualifying physical, hearing, or psychiatric disability.

Sweet Melissa Fund
http://sweetmelissafund.org/
Lung Transplant, Lung Transplant
Provides financial assistance to lung transplant patients.

Sy's Fund
http://sysfund.org/application/
Cancer - All
Provides financial assistance to young adults with cancer to pursue their passions or complementary treatments.

The Gift of Sunshine (TGOS) - The Hope Chest
http://www.thegiftofsunshine.org/hopechest.html
Disability
Provides financial assistance towards obtaining a service dog.

This Star Won't Go Out
http://tswgo.org/financial-assistance.html
Childhood Cancer
Provides financial assistance to families with a child who has cancer.

Tigerlily Foundation - Funds for Families Program
http://tigerlilyfoundation.org/programs/support/funds-for-families-program/
Breast Cancer
Provides financial assistance to families with a member having breast cancer.

Tinina Q. Cade Foundation, Inc. - Family Building Grant
http://www.cadefoundation.org/Grants/family-building-grant
Infertility
Provides financial assistance for treatment for individuals who have infertility.

United Breast Cancer Foundation (UBCF) - Breast Screening
http://www.ubcf.info/breast-screening/
Breast Cancer
Provides screenings to women who are at risk for breast cancer.

United Breast Cancer Foundation (UBCF) - Individual Grant Program
http://www.ubcf.info/individual-grant/
Breast Cancer
Provides customized financial assistance to individuals who have breast cancer.

United Breast Cancer Foundation (UBCF) - Reconstructive Surgery Grant Program
http://www.ubcf.info/breast-reconstruction/
Breast Cancer
Provides financial assistance for reconstructive surgery for women who have had a mastectomy through the treatment of breast cancer.

United States Department of Veterans Affairs - VA Caregiver Support Services
http://www.caregiver.va.gov/support/support_services.asp
Disability, Chronic, Serious or Life Threatening Illnesses, All Diseases
Provides services to assist family caregivers of veterans.

Variety: the Children's Charity - Kids on the Go!
http://www.usvariety.org/programs.html
Disability - Childhood, Childhood Disability, Disability Requiring Assistive Technology
Provides financial assistance for goods and services to children who have disabilities.

Verna's Purse

http://www.reprotech.com/financial-assistance.html?faqitem=faq31

Cancer - All

Provides financial assistance to young adults pursuing fertility preservation necessitated by a recent cancer diagnosis or treatment.

Walk On Foundation, Inc.

http://www.walkonfoundation.com/

Medical Condition Requiring Hospitalization, Disability Requiring Assistive Technology

Provides financial and other types of assistance to individuals and families related to medical hospitalization.

Walking With Anthony

http://www.walkingwithanthony.org/mission/our-mission/

Spinal Cord Injuries, Spinal Cord Injuries

Provides financial assistance to individuals with spinal cord injury

Waner Children's Vascular Anomaly Foundation

http://www.wanerkids.org/financial

Vascular Anomaly

Provides financial assistance for children with vascular anomaly.

Warrior Canine Connection

http://warriorcanineconnection.org/

Assistance Dog, Mobility Disability, Post-traumatic Stress Disorder, Traumatic Brain Injury, Traumatic Brain Injury, Amputation, Disability - Mobility, Post-traumatic Stress Disorder

Warrior Canine Connection enlists recovering service members with PTSD in a therapeutic mission of learning how to train service dogs for their fellow veterans with physical disabilities.

Wheel to Walk Foundation

http://www.wheeltowalk.com/index.htm

Disability, Disability, Disability Requiring Assistive Technology

Provides financial assistance for assistive technology devices and/or services to children who have a disability.

Wheelchair Recycler

http://wheelchairrecycler.org/

Conditions Requiring Medical Equipment, Disability, Wheelchair Bound

Provides free or low cost reconditioned wheelchairs.

Women's Reproductive Assistance Project

http://www.wrrap.org/about-wrrap/

Unwanted Pregnancy

Provides financial assistance to women who are seeking to terminate an unwanted pregnancy.

Xenazine Medication Assistance Program - REACH (Resources, Education and Access for patients with Chorea associated with Huntington's disease)
http://www.xenazineusa.com/FinancialHelp

ZERO: The End of Prostate Cancer - Prostate Cancer Drive
http://zerocancer.org/testing/testing-map
Prostate Cancer
Provides prostate cancer screenings for men who are at risk.